long

Sounds &
Letters 21

o

T0025474

**KNOWLEDGE
BOOKS**

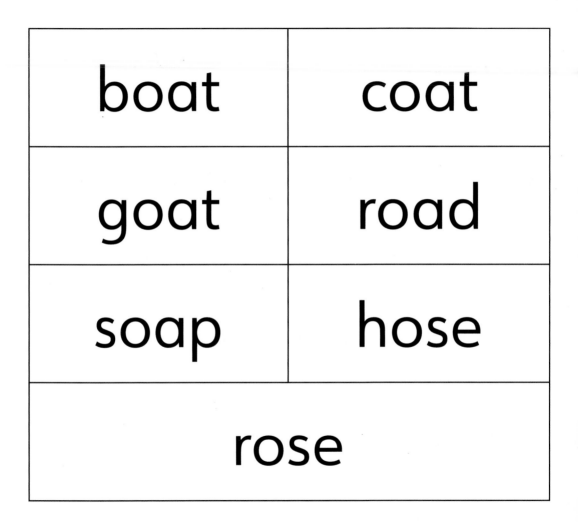

boat	coat
goat	road
soap	hose
rose	

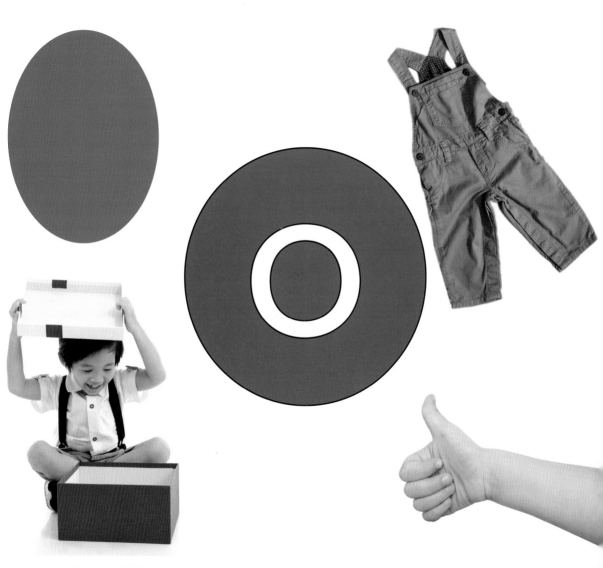

boat

coat

5

goat

road

9

soap

hose

rose

boat	coat
goat	road
soap	hose
rose	

Knowledge Books and Software
PO Box 50 Sandgate, Queensland 4017 Australia
p. +617-55680288 f. +617-55680277 email: sales@kbs.com.au

First Published 2022
ISBN 9781922516930
Text and editing: Carole Crimeen
Design and layout: Suzanne Fletcher
Publisher: Robert Watts

Series Information: **Sounds and Letters**

Credits

Photographs: Cover © wee dezign; p. 1 © gcafotografia, ANURAK PONGPATIMET, Vitalinka; p. 3 © richard pross; p. 5 © urfin; p. 7 © Eric Isselee; p. 9 © ver0nicka; p. 11 © oksana2010; p. 13 © eurobanks; p. 15 © Tiger Images/Shutterstock.

Phonic support books are a wonderful resource for emergent readers as they encourage independent reading and help students make the link between letters and the sounds they represent.

Have students identify the images on the title page to listen for the long or short vowel sound that they will hear through the book.

Encourage students to point to each word as they read through the book.

ISBN: 9781922516930

9 781922 516930 >

KNOWLEDGE BOOKS

Sounds&Letters